Crannóg 51 summer 2019

Editorial Board

Sandra Bunting
Ger Burke
Jarlath Fahy
Tony O'Dwyer

ISSN 1649-4865
ISBN 978-1-907017-54-4

Cover image: *'Charon'*, by Róisín Coyle
Cover image sourced by Sandra Bunting
Cover design by Wordsonthestreet
Published by Wordsonthestreet for Crannóg magazine
www.wordsonthestreet.com   @wordsstreet

CONTENTS

Submissions for Crannóg 52 open November 1st until November 30th
Publication date is March 6th 2020

Crannóg is published bi-annually in spring and autumn.

*Submission Times: Month of **November** for spring issue. Month of **May** for autumn issue.*

We will <u>not read</u> submissions sent outside these times.

POETRY: Send no more than three poems. Each poem should be under 50 lines.

PROSE: Send one story. Stories should be under 2,000 words.

We do not accept postal submissions.

*When emailing your submission we require **three** things:*

1. *The text of your submission included both in body of email and as a Word attachment (this is to ensure correct layout. We may, however, change your layout to suit our publication).*

2. *A brief bio in the third person. Include this both in body and in attachment.*

3. *A postal address for contributor's copy in the event of publication.*

For full submission details, to learn more about Crannóg Magazine, to purchase copies of the current issue, or take out a subscription, log on to our website:

www.crannogmagazine.com

Poetry in Motion

Maria Kenny

YEATS, KAVANAGH, HEANEY? Don't make me laugh. Boring old dead poets. *No Second Troy* about Ireland? Eh, the clue's in the title – 'Troy'? *Stony Grey Soil* only made me determined to go nowhere as boring as Monaghan and as for *Mid-Term Break,* sooooo depressing. Shite, the lot of it, and those who think they're cool, who quote the poems .... Especially at weddings – 'Had I the Heavens....'

Real poetry is on the streets. Like Mad Maggie who's always hanging around the shops.

'Gis a few euro, love, help an old woman out.'

Same song every day. One time, Deano threw a two-euro coin at her. It bounced off the side of her head and she picked it up and said 'thanks'. Man, I thought I was going to die laughing. It nearly took her eye out and she's thanking him. Poor old wagon, she sings when she talks, she's worse when she's high, but hilarious. We go up and talk to her, ask her about her family. She loves talking about her kids that were taken off her.

'Maggie, how's your kids?'

And she goes quiet, eyes us, because she knows we're only taking the piss.

'Maggie, how's your daughter? I think I saw her at the shops.'

Every - fucking - time she falls for it.

'You saw my Melanie?'

Deano is great at it.

'Yeah,' he says, 'if it wasn't her, it was someone the image of you.'

'Did she look good?'

'She looked dynamite, Maggie.'

'I'm gonna get my kids back, gonna get clean. There's programs...'

'Yeah Maggie, not for you though. Your daughter... she said her mam is dead.'

And then Maggie starts her whinging. It's so funny. She falls for it all the time.

'Ah Maggie shut up,' Deano says to her. 'Shut up and I'll give you a few euro.'

She's like my baby brother when he's trying not to cry. Her lip is all wobbly and her eyes are leaking like mad. Its hard not to laugh. Deano's so bad, but it's funny. Maggie there trying to stop her crying for a couple of euros. She does okay out of it. We all give her our odds, so it's not like she isn't getting paid for the entertainment.

How come all these great poets don't write about that? Where's the poems about the needles hanging out of legs of grown men, or worse. Though that's funny too. This guy had his trousers down, injecting the top of his thigh and Deano runs up and robs his haversack. The poor guy was trying to pull his trousers up while the needle was still in him. He was so confused. I was still laughing that night in bed.

I did hear this poet though, he came into our class trying to get us to get into writing and stuff. He read a few of his poems, but it was more like rap. His arms were flying all over the place and at first it was funny but he was talking about his girlfriend who was a junkie and how he loved her. The whole class was listening and no one even sniggered when he cursed. I looked over at Miss Donoghue, but she was watching him like he was a god or something. After, he got us to try it. Martina Holmes read out hers and he told her it was great, but it wasn't. It was about her younger sister who has something mentally wrong with her, she gets the special bus to the spa school. The poet guy told her she was very brave to tackle something so raw to her, his exact words. We ripped the piss out of her in maths class.

I liked him though and later that night when I finally got my two sisters to sleep, I tried to write something real proper like. It wasn't much use, but I felt proud of it. I wanted to show Miss Donoghue, but I was too scared someone else would see it.

My poem was about this oul lad that does be on the canal. His name is Jimmy and he's ancient but he's not old in the way he goes on. He's not like the other drunks along the canal. I was on the hop one day, walking down the canal, cause any adult would shit themselves along there, so I knew it was safe enough.

'You on the mitch?' Jimmy said to me as I walked past and I don't know what it was, maybe it was the argument I had with mam that morning, or just the whole fucked-up-ness of everything, but I stopped to talk to him. I looked around first though, just in case any of the others were on the hop too and saw me.

'I am, yeah. What's it to you?' I said.

I kept my hands in my pockets and kind of leaned on one leg, the way Niamh O'Connor does when she's giving it loads.

'Education is important, I should know. I didn't have any. You'll end up like me if you don't go to school,' he said.

I rolled my eyes. I just felt weary.

'Why don't you sit down, love?' he said and I gave him a look, you know, a 'you gonna try anything' look.

He laughed and told me again to sit down.

I plonked on the bench beside him, keeping my hands in my pockets.

'Jimmy,' he said reaching his hand out to me.

I looked at his hand for a bit, then sighing I shook his hand.

'Audrey,' I said.

'Nice to meet you. And tell me, Audrey, what brings you out here when you should be at school?'

'School is a load of shite. They teach you nothing that you need for the real world. What use is knowing every river in the world?'

'For travelling.'

'And why do I need to know all about the Irish Constitution?'

'It's your history, your culture.'

'And poetry? What do I need poetry for?'

'Ah,' he said, sitting back and folding his arms. 'Would you have a ciggie?' he asked.

I stared at him for a moment but he didn't look away. The box was sticking out of my pocket so he didn't need to ask. Sighing as loudly as I could, I gave him one.

'You're a good skin,' he said putting it behind his ear.

I lit one up myself.

'We are an island of saints and scholars,' he said, looking at the swans as they glided by.

'You're right of course, poetry mightn't help you much through life but when it does, you'll never look back. You heard that saying "chicken soup for the soul"? Well, that's American shite. Poetry is what feeds your soul.'

'It's all bull, I don't understand a word of it,' I said. 'You read it and find out it's not even what you thought it was about. They're writing about going for a walk and it's about life-changing decisions? Why don't they just say that instead of all the bullshit? Stupid.'

I took a deep drag of my cigarette. He was eyeing it.

'Fuck sake,' I said, and passed it to him.

'Much obliged,' he said.

Smoke escaped from his mouth as he continued.

'Thing is, the whole beauty of poetry is what you find in it. You might see a guy going for a walk and that's enough for you, but someone else might see something completely different.'

'Yeah but if I want to pass my exams, I have to know that shit.'

'When you get the rhythm of poetry, you'll see the clear meaning.'

'Yeah, right. I can't understand a bleeding word they're talking about. Why do they use so many stupid big words?'

'It's the beat,' he said.

'What?'

'*Because I could not stop for death – it kindly stopped for me – The Carriage held but just Ourselves – And Immortality,*' he said, slapping his thigh to the rhythm. 'You hear it?'

And I did. I liked that poem, all her poems. Something Dickinson. She was dark, gothic. Real 'American Horror Story' shit.

'I hear it,' I said trying not to smile.

'It's all there if you listen.'

We sat in silence for a while and it was nice, comfortable.

'What do you want to do when you leave school?' he said after a while.

'Dunno, haven't really thought about it.'

'You must want to do something?'

'I'm probably going to leave after the Junior Cert to be honest.'

He turned on the bench to look at me.

'Why?'

'Huh? Because... I don't know. I'm crap at school.'

'What would you love to do if you could do anything?'

I smiled. 'I'd be rich and famous, no worries.'

Jimmy laughed. 'Okay, but if you had to pick a real job?'

I folded my arms and watched the Luas go by. 'I don't know... maybe work with animals. When I was younger I wanted to be a vet or something.'

'How old are you now?'

'Fifteen.'

'You can still be a vet.'

This time I laughed. 'Eh yeah? I told you, I'm shite at school.'

'But if you tried? You are at that amazing age where you can be anything. An astronaut, a fireman, president of the country.'

'Will you stop,' I said taking two cigarettes out of the box. I handed him one and he nodded his thanks at me.

'If you put your mind to it and the work in?'

I thought of Miss Donoghue then. She was always going on about my potential and how I was wasting it.

'I'd be laughed out of it by my mates if I got all nerdy,' I said.

'Sure how would they know?' he said, tapping the side of his nose. 'You study at home, you listen in school.'

'Have you been in my house?' I said, thinking of that morning and mam screaming up the road after me, the baby in her arms, reaching for me, bawling his little eyes out because I wouldn't take him. 'Anyway, they'd know in school if I kept passing tests.'

'You must be good if you know you could pass them. You play smart, brush it off, laugh it off as if it's nothing and all the while, work hard, get your points for college and get out of here,' he said.

I looked around. On sunny days it was nice, but really it was a kip of grey concrete flats that we called apartments to make us sound less poor.

'I don't think I'd cope with college.'

'Course you would.'

'You don't even know me,' I said, looking at him.

'I do,' he said, all serious. 'I have a gift. I can see people for what they are and you, Audrey, you're better than the life you're laying out for yourself.'

I had to look away. 'I'll think about it,' I said standing up.

'Do,' he said, stubbing his cigarette.

'You're not bad for an old lad,' I said.

'Tell that to your mates.'

I looked at the ground. Even though I didn't do anything to him, I was there when the others robbed his bag or drink.

'See you around, Jimmy,' I said, walking off.

I tucked the poem into my pillowcase after I had written it. When everyone was asleep, I took it out again and read it and before I chickened out, I looked up the points needed to be a vet.

The next morning, I met up with the gang and we walked to school together. Everyone gave us a wide berth.

This was the life. Respect was more important than anything. College was for poets. As we walked, I thought of Jimmy's words to me as I had left him.

'Take care now, Audrey. Look for the path less travelled and take it,' he had said.

I waved a goodbye to him, though I hadn't a clue what he was talking about.

Hem

Cian Ferriter

Evenings when
you were not yet back
I'd sit on the makeshift
bench in the yard

of our first house
where you'd hung
a line with room
for just one dress

and close my eyes
and wait for the breeze
to lift your hem
against my knees.

The Third Anniversary

Catriona Clutterbuck

This stone
is becoming pliable,
like warmed putty
pinched soft,
its outer layers giving
the fingers plenty to do,
but leadened,
fit for the pockets
of one looking at a river

or like the stone I need,
blunt yet heavy,
to place at the bottom
of the vase of white
double-headed narcissi,
drunken-scented
from the garden,
that I would leave
at my daughter's grave
on her third anniversary,
to stop the wind
blowing it over.

Part & Parcel

Susan Tepper

Close the shutters
Allow darkness to rip
Your eyes in tide pools.

Two suitcases, side by side
Have yet to be unpacked.

Excuses, elaborations
Does this mean we won't stay long?

You're flattened by so many roads
I am stung and run over.

Two suitcases: it's been written
Part & Parcel by your own hand.

Hail Marys

Máiríde Woods

Those first grown-up years
you left the Hail Marys at home
lodged in a purse from someone else's
trip to Lourdes. But they followed you
along the broad and shining path
disguising the hour of our death.
Now you're grateful they stayed
the course, refused rebuffs. When
the first clay falls on the coffin
they gabble themselves.

Other women called Mary
take your arm. They know
how to shelter figures
in newly borrowed black coats,
people like you who've lost
men and mothers and dreams.
Now and then grace bursts out
from between clouds and wizened trees
reminding you of the possibility
of fruitfulness

The final chapter takes place
on one of those blue, symmetrical hills
– straight from a Giotto painting.
The Lord, though somewhere within,
plays hard to get, reluctant to commit ...
absorbed in his divinity, I surmise.
As the olive harvest shrinks,
you stake out patience
and wait for a shard of grace
nam*ed Maria.*

Ancient

Tatjana Mirkov-Popovicki

I REGRET THAT I DON'T HAVE MUCH WISDOM to impart at this point in my Iliadic life, but the one thing I can tell you is how it feels to be one hundred years old.

The first thing you'll want to know is that I still have dreams of intimacy. I've dreamed of my dear wife, my Penelope with lingonberry lips and nipples, even when I was far away, just as most husbands do, and all husbands say they do.

With that fact out of the way, let me try to depict how a person of my age experiences the pandemonium of the external world.

My body, neatly packed in a wheelchair, is a haphazardly assembled collection of small oddly shaped parts that used to fit well together before they got worn out and wonky.

For my sight, I thank the miracles of optometry but the hearing is a whole other game. The contraptions which used to do the trick a quarter of a century ago now fail me. But I've learned to adapt and my shortcoming became a source of amusement. Deciphering my family's conversations has become a welcome distraction from aches and pains. Examples abound.

What I hear as a faint *gun pa*, means someone is yelling *grandpa* in my ear. One of my favourites, *long ah*, uttered by my day nurse, a slender thing with curiously cool hands, means I am headed toward a heavenly *sponge bath*. You'd be surprised how much pleasure can be had in my condition.

Just this morning, my dear Penelope, an eighty-year-old master of the Internet, bangs her fists on the keyboard and throws her spectacles in despair. The cat escapes from her lap.

'*Umph uterus,*' she shrieks. I know that one well, but it never gets old. She *hates computers*. Still, she often exchanges emails with family and friends.

'*Sonya as good noose.*' She won't say anything else. Our favourite great-granddaughter is bringing her new fellow for the first meet and greet. Penelope says Sonya wants to tell me the *good noose* herself. For me, the good news is that I am still alive and that I have my dear wife at my side. That all the kids are well, raised to be the good people they are. For all that, the credit goes to Penelope, although that isn't her real name.

Her real name is Riitta, but she became Penelope when I returned home from a three-year hiatus and found her peeling potatoes in the kitchen of our cabin on the west coast of Canada. We had been enthusiastically, vigorously, and regularly trying to conceive for a number of years, and one morning on my way to work, feeling a certain void and enormous fatigue, I walked by a Greyhound depot and realised I wanted to see the rest of Canada. So I did just that. I hopped on the bus and ventured east. I sent Riitta cards from every town I went through and I told her where I was headed next. She never wrote back but she always made sure there was money in our bank account. When I reached the Atlantic Ocean via a tiny village in Newfoundland named Dildo, I felt a strong urge to return to my wife. I was relieved to find her peeling potatoes.

'My dear Penelope,' I said, tears welling in my eyes. 'You waited for me.'

'I'll get more spuds,' Penelope said. 'How was Canada?'

'Very chilly in the north.'

The next day we filed for adoption and soon we got Ben, a sweet three-year-old boy, skinny like a mouse. Then we got Gina and Stan, the twins, and later a few more. We now stand strong at six kids, thirteen grandkids, twenty-two of the youngest ones, and still counting. We have artists, writers, and teachers in the family. My favourite baby girl, Sonya, is a scientist – a geneticist no less. My role in all this success is minor. I help by cheering on, giving praise and the little things they need and I happen to be able to provide.

The other day, Sonya asked for my spit. How lucky I was to still have something useful to give. She said it was possible to trace the history of my family that way. Penelope asked if they needed my other bodily fluids for such a grand exploration. I'll spare you the process of communicating all this through my aged ears, but I must mention that among all her immense natural qualities, humour isn't Penelope's strong suit. She was right about one thing, though. Tracing the history of my family would indeed be a great adventure.

You see, my old man was an orphan. He enlisted at the age of fifteen and the end of the First World War found him in Greece, where he met my mother, a dark-eyed Balkan refugee of ambiguous origin, who said 'yes' to anything he'd asked of her. It turned out that she was generally an agreeable woman, and after I was born, she said 'yes' to a British officer who promised her a better life than Dad could ever offer. I was a wee babe when he brought me to Canada, but I fancy I can still remember the vast blueness of the Aegean Sea and that exquisite Mediterranean light glistening on the silky undulating waves.

Dad instilled in me a passion for Greek mythology. You see, for all the years of his growing up, he yearned to know his family. He wondered who he was, which nationality he could claim as his own. But Greece had changed him.

'I saw the humanity,' he said to me many times, a tear trailing down his wrinkled cheek. He talked about the masses of starved soldiers and refugees, peoples of many European nations crammed on the beaches of the great sea, waiting to sail to whichever country would take them.

'Remember this, my son,' he said. 'Everyone came from somewhere, and lacking the exact source of origin, Ancient Greece is a fine supplement to one's native land.'

He told me the tales of Greek gods and goddesses and I came to think of Odysseus and Agamemnon as my brothers. I knew the *Iliad* by heart before I could write.

It's not good for me to sink so deep into memories because I fear that one day, I won't find my way back to my Penelope. This afternoon, I woke from my nap with a foggy mind, slipping back to my dream of Erebus descending from Mount Olympus on a cottony cloud. Penelope made her staple lingonberry pie for Sonya and her strapping fellow, whose name is Barry.

'*Err*,' he grunts and clumsily settles at the dining table, next to my wheelchair.

'*Be-rry*,' squeals Sonya into my ear.

'*Lick'm berry*,' says Penelope and hands Barry a plate with a humongous slice of pie dripping with thick maroon sauce.

At first, I take the tattoo on his right bicep for a smudge of dirt, but it's a picture of a horse with words 'Free Chilcotin' below it. A horse-lover! This cheers me up.

'Do you know Trojans, son?' I ask enthusiastically. He glances at Sonya and looks confused. His lack of familiarity with Ancient Greece doesn't bother me because the story of the Trojan horse is a fine tale and I would very much enjoy sharing it with him. But Sonya and Penelope are restless.

'Good noose, good noose,' they shout. But now I am thinking of Trojans, the battles to reclaim Helen of Troy, and pools of blood soaking into the gritty sand.

'Good news for you, darling,' says Penelope with odd clarity and smiles at me so sweetly, I see her the way she was many years ago. Her gentle face looks smooth and young and I forget for a moment how old we both are.

'What is it?' I ask. 'Are you pregnant?'

Just as I say this, my feet sink into the warm sand, crystalline water lapping my ankles.

They all laugh. Sonya shakes some papers and spreads them on the table. Their voices curdle in my ears.

'*You prick*,' Sonya says and stabs the papers with her finger.

'*You freak*.' Penelope hugs me.

'*You reek*.' Barry grins at me.

I don't know what they are trying to say. My head hurts, my chest aches. Only my feet feel light and cool, gently massaged by the ebb and flow of waves.

'*Ga, ga, ga, reek*,' Penelope makes gagging sounds, and that does it.

'Oh, am I?' I cry out. 'Is that possible?'

'Yes, brother, you are one of us,' says Odysseus and extends his muscular arm to hoist me onto his fine raft. The sea is placid and green but a mass of purple feathery storm clouds gather on the horizon. The golden ribbon between heaven and earth slowly fades. It will soon disappear. The breeze smells like seaweed and urchins.

Odysseus gazes at me approvingly and points at the tattoo on his forearm. It's a simple heart pierced by an arrow and above it, it says 'Penelope'. Oh, how I wish I had one just like that.

Seoul

Laura Treacy Bentley

A monk appeared in dreams from time to time.
He gave me an apple and this kept my hope alive.
                    Park Seung-hyung

Sixteen days without food or drink,
not even rainwater,
entombed beneath the rubble
of five stories
and six hundred bodies,
Park waited.

She whispered through concrete slabs
until her words
became moans,
then silence.

Sixteen nights he left his temple
of flowers and incense
to walk the black sands,
a staff in one hand,
an apple in the other.

Each night he offered it.
Each night it turned red
in her hand.

Rescuers found Park alive.
They brought doctors and drugs,
water and rice,
but she had no pain,
no hunger.

Swathed only in a blanket
with a red towel to protect her eyes,
she asked for an apple,
a gift for a monk.

A Reckoning

Kevin Higgins

---

after Christina Rosetti

My lungs are an accordion fallen out of tune
playing an air I've grown too used to.
Pour me tall glass after tall glass of summer sea air;
let me gulp them down with sliced strawberries.
My lungs belong in a shop
that sells second-hand bagpipes to the gullible.
May the cigarette smoke and diesel fumes of others
(and the mould and stress I brought to the table myself)
all be detained in the lamp-lit interrogation room
I'm building without planning permission
at the bottom of the garden.

My lungs are two talentless divas
competing with each other for newspaper headlines.
May everyone be arrested without warrant
and made plead.
Because the bill for my life is on the mat.
My lungs are rooms in which the yellow
wallpaper is slowly falling down.
My hates have come to get me
and are busy printing the word guilty on every
piece of paper they can find.

The Serrated Shadow

Deborah Moffatt

Time stalls at the back of the byre,
a black shadow falling on long wet grass,

the undulant line of the pan-tiled roof
reflected on flat ground,

a serrated edge severing night from day,
past from present, dark from light,

the land divided, the black and the green,
the myth and the illusion,

you, alone, your back to the wall,
salt weeping from lime and stone,

a memory of sweat in blood and bone,
of reap and sow, of harvest, of home,

night fading, the shadow line slicing
sharp and fine through time.

Cassandra

Beate Sigriddaughter

When I am alone I play
the flute. I have given up
on spoken words. No one believes
me anyway in this daunting
invisibility. My flute remembers
the past. Also the future. I am
not often alone.

This is after the rape. I remember
Ajax, in Athena's temple, raping
me. Everyone else, including Athena,
indignantly helpless. I remember
Apollo cursing me, spitting
into my mouth long before that
because I wouldn't give him the sex
he wanted and claims I promised.
I didn't of course. Just having
a woman's body is not a promise.
He didn't get that. I remember
the future. Thousands of years
down the road a wise woman will
explain: that's what you get, yes,
when you refuse a god. I know.

I knew what would happen. Soon
I will be killed with Agamemnon,
whose concubine I am. That, too,
against my will, the spoils of war.

I play the flute when I can.

Had I known all this when I refused
the god and unrequited lust,
would I still have said no? You see,
I always did know. You know it too.
My word was no. They didn't like it.
God curses, men take what they want.

I play my flute into the future.
Make me a better world, I beg of
you. Try harder.

Caretaker of the Callows

Laura Ann Caffrey

---

for Seán

In late spring and early summer, he rows
the small wooden boat to Inishee, across
a narrow run of Shannon waters
from mainland to island
to mend fences.

Ashore, he wades through meadow grasses, sedge
and water mint, the greater nest in which
lapwing, redshank and curlew call
and choose to perform the precarious task
of raising their young.

All day he works on wire and electric cables
the boundary between the delicate
manoeuvrings of avian life and
the hungry traipsing of larger beings.
This fence

a freedom in confines, is never done –
cattle scratching bend the fence too low, or
scrub growth compromises the current, so
he must work, strengthening, reconnecting

protecting these unknowing birds until
light fades

and he can work no more. He downs his tools,
makes his way back, only to find some creature
has gnawed through cable back where he started.
It is work for tomorrow where
there are always more fences to mend.

The Space between Matter

Kirsten McKenzie

THOSE WERE THE DAYS OF SCORCHED SKIN and porcelain skies. Days when we lived on the beach, beyond the melting sun and into the dark. We talked of space and time, of the space between matter, and we smoked your crazy strong weed until our eyes rolled back in our heads and our brain cells fizzed into nothingness like Mentos in Coke.

You talked of physics and I talked of poetry. Blake, mainly, grains of sand, doors of perception, that kind of thing. If a thing loves, you read from my little book, it is infinite. You told me about your dream; your life's purpose, extracting energy from the space between the atoms. I extracted energy from the space where you had been, the smell of your clothes, leftover cups of coffee, the taste of your lips on the damp paper edge of your joint.

You were beautiful, of course. Beauty and truth were as easy to come by in those days as peachy dusks and hash and sex and sleep. We spoke in concepts, love and desire and time and infinity. We were all beautiful then, if only we'd known it.

A star was born. Stella. You looked into my eyes and I saw stars there too, flickering the way they did the night Stella was conceived. On and off. The funny thing is, you said, half of them aren't even there anymore.

In the sitting room I watched Stella gurgle into her muslins and cleaned her tarry poo. Her gaping mouth rooted for my breast like a blind worm, reaching out for life, while my own life contracted, darkened.

When black holes contract they result in powerful nuclear explosions, you said. They release skull-splitting energy.

You were not talking to me. Your voice came from the cupboard you called your office, where you sat with the man you called your associate. An old professor, a lonely man, I could tell from his expression and the sour smell of his clothes, but you said he was a genius, and who was I to disagree? You liked to take in the rejects, the waifs and strays. They were attracted to your sparkling brilliance, just like I had been.

Had been. I fed Stella in the warmth of the sun's rays, in the little sitting room. Folded the muslin over her mouth as the smoke curled from the place where your voice was. You talked of cold fusion and zero-point energy and I dreamt of days we would spend with Stella, when your project was done, watching her grow in space and time.

More people came and went. Academics, mostly, PhD students, techy entrepreneurs. Dreamers like you. You had a way of making them feel special. You bought more computers, several screens set up side by side, and you nursed the egos of dreamers from across the world. It wouldn't be long, you told me, not long now. You were waiting for the funding to come through. I waited for Stella to fall asleep. The health visitor gave me the benefits forms, and I filled them in. I'm good at filling in forms, I told her. That's nice, dear, she said. Here's another two.

I filled in the forms, while you talked in your little room about the cosmos, crystals by your laptop. Winter came, and I walked by the dark water in the crystal air, breathing it in. The sky still scattered light towards me, but it was swollen and grey, like the lids of my eyes.

Christmas Day and the money had not come. I walked with Stella to the beach. I met you, coming the other way. You'd said you didn't want to come. I smiled, opening my mouth to thank you. To thank you for changing your mind. But you didn't see me at all. Your eyes fixed to the sky. Your skin the colour of clay. You were already gone.

Easter, and Stella learned to roll. I watched her roll, over and over, and my laugh was her laugh. Look, I said. Look at her roll. You looked. And you smiled. But your eyes were uncertain. Babies roll, you were thinking. Your mind was on higher things.

A phone call at last. The money was on its way. This was it, and your eyes lit again. Everything you'd ever dreamed of. You laughed. The baby laughed. I laughed.

Weeks passed. They'll do it by transfer, you said. Bitcoin. These people don't work in cash. I suggested a job, a part-time thing. I used to waitress. I could do it again. Tide us over 'til the money .... But the money was coming, you interrupted. Didn't I believe you? And what about Stella? How could I take care of her if I worked?

Well, I had thought that you were working at home ....

Take care of a baby? While I bring about the most important ... I mean ... what the hell is it you think I do?

Honestly, I had no idea. I had no idea what you did.

Don't you think it's time? I said. Time to move on. Do something different?

You turned to me. Your pupils black holes in a dark sky. A sign of attraction, I'd read, to something. But not to me. Different, yes. Exopolitics, you said. That's the next big thing.

Exo – what?

That's where the struggle is now, you said. That's why the money hadn't come through. They were doing everything in their power to stop it.

We won't let them, you said. We won't let them destroy us.

Stella picked up a crushed breadstick from the floor, covered in hair. I pulled it from her damp fingers.

You were in that mood now, darting, fast. Love, I've got to go. And you kissed me, your eyes alight with it again, whatever it was.

Dadda away, said Stella, pointing to the door. She put her hands out and looked from side to side. Where dadda gone? She thought it was a game.

The phone rang a lot. You were involved in it all. Something big, you said. Bigger than anything the world has ever seen. Intergalactic. Warfare. It had to be stopped.

Stella was, rarely, sleeping. Intergalactic? You mean, like, between planets?

Exactly! You've got it, babe. Right on the nose. You touched my nose, then. Pleased with me. I've said the right thing, and I should be pleased with myself too.

When we first met you were that hippy on the beach. You said things about water and air and space and how everything in the world was one. How we were one, just two parts of one whole. We were the space between matter. We mattered. I mattered. I needed to matter then. Now Stella looks up at me and I know that you are the space and I am the matter.

Later, on the beach, Stella picks the sand up and rubs it in my hair, laughing again. She never stops laughing, Stella. No matter what.

Mummy phone, mummy phone. She stretches out her hands.

Not just now, not mummy phone. This is important, Stella, sshh, mummy needs to speak to the man.

You always liked to stick it to the man. That was your style. But now you needed to listen to the man. He came and he saw your grey face and he said that you needed to take some time, some space, to work things out.

What do you know of space and time, you said. What do you know of the space between matter, of the energy all around us, of the time running out, running down? So little time left before they come for us. And we're the only things doing anything about it. I am. The only. One.

Who? the man asked. Are they? He was only a little older than us, with blond hair and kind eyes. He wore a wedding ring.

The phone rang. You answered it. Yeah, they've sent one of their representatives. He's here right now. I know. Your eyes flickered up the blond man, scanning up and down.

You think so?

You'd started to pace with the phone. I know, sure, OK, yes, I agree, it's the best course. The only course. Pacing and pacing. Your fingers curled into your palms and I'd seen it before, that action, just a few months before, that time I took Stella out and didn't tell you first where I was going. It was only because I was so worried, you said. It's my job to protect you, you said. You and Stella. You are my world. My universe. My infinite love.

The blond man was making some notes. A prescription, he said, I think may help.

I think it would help if you left, I said.

When you came out of the kitchen, clutching the knife, the corners of your eyes were pink.

You don't know who I am, you said. I'm not from here.

I know, I said. You're from Melbourne. I tried to work out, from your expression, what you could recall. How much of you was still part of us.

But your pupils had disintegrated in your eyes. Tiny specks of dust floating in grey space. You know they sent him, you said.

I told you I know. I didn't tell you I was one of them, now. Your gravity was weakening. I was being pulled away by forces larger than both of us.

I was near the door, had picked up Stella. I'd learned to do these things without thinking.

We go to the beach, Stella and I. I tell her about land and sea and air and space and matter. How much she matters to me. How she is my world, my love. My infinite universe. She is my sun and I am her earth, and you a retreating, dying star, blinking out there in the dark sky. From time to time I will look at you, but I know that every day your halo will dim, and you will retreat a little further away, until the day you implode, scattering your debris into the universe. At least then you'll have achieved your aim, releasing energy from the space between matter.

Now That You Are Gone

Ria Collins

In memory of my mother

The crows in the belfry croak their chilled call,
the clouds above shudder with cold.

I left you looking for me across stars at night,
throwing holy water that fell to the ground

while I rode camels through the desert
escaping the parched boredom

like a balloonist
distant and removed, in motion.

My letters neatly ordered in a drawer,
I trace unguent Vicks and pills and half used face cream,

touch worn rosary-beads and medals,
hair strands in your comb,

pink lipstick almost used,
lace handkerchief in a drooping pocket

of your worn and faded gown
perfumed with lavender,

the new one I gave you neatly folded
amongst the unused thermal vests.

Torn out pages of recipes
spill like bruised memories across a blue pain,

sometimes I pretend you are still here
labelling warm marmalade jars in the kitchen.

The younger you full of laughter
chasing us out to school after breakfast

of porridge and Clonakilty black pudding,
is a faded make-believe in ochre.

Yes you pushed your self-righteous
exhausted torrent of despair on us,

when I travelled the distance to visit,
five days invariably became two,

but I miss you like an amputated limb
that burns and stings with real imaginings.

The bell peals for Mass and the rooks take flight,
rain pours, I hide in your room ; unseen.

It will pass as all things, leaving only
its scent behind, a lingering trace of having been.

Putting a Face to Limerick

Mary Melvin Geoghegan

in the Hunt Museum

a miniature Viking hammer

nails the photo of Honora Walsh

as she could or might have been

before, lost on a famine ship

created by the artist Beth Nagle.

Later, in St. Mary's Cathedral

there's a holding of breath

at a dusty opening on the north transept

where lepers in medieval times

were allowed to receive communion.

And round the corner at King John's Castle

the burden of occupation

from Viking, Norman and English times

is as solid as the enormous stone battlements

that keep the Shannon out.

There and Here

Gail Anderson

HE IS AWAKE, WALKING, LEAVING HIS RADIO, the shipping forecast. Fisher, Dogger. Dawn flat as pewter, a fag in his lips. His grip on the match shows dogwhelk fists, pied, palsied.

He fills these empty streets with ghosts. There, the talkative midwife, there the grocer, fishmonger, sailmaker. Creels and floats, cats herring-hungry, flower-boxed sills, there laundry, there nets line-drying ....

Snow swirls like moths, salt-silver, slicking the road. Cold moves him onward. Each day, each night is the same. Waking, walking, drifting as the moon and sun slip from cloud to cloud, handing the days between them.

In the aquarium warmth of the cafe, open early though no one comes, the oilcloth under his elbows will smell of bleach. He will nurse his coffee, watch the dawn come, watch the sea shake and shoulder the breakwater, watch wisps of haar along the vacant quayside.

At the top of Ship Street he stops. Below, the cafe window burns yellow in darkness, and he sees them there, at his table. Remembers the town's tutting. *Incomers, strangers.* One black, one white, unmarried, they have rented the old cinema, the Electric, pulled the boards from its doors. The man's dark curls, the woman's bare shoulders shine like pearls in a jeweller's window.

When the bell on the cafe door rings him in, they don't look. The man eyes the ceiling. The woman gazes down at the pavement outside, lips pressed to the crook of a finger. He takes a new table, one with no cloth, its wood etched with faint figures. *5, 12, fish, dog.* A long-ago child, pen-pressing thin paper.

If I sit here long enough, he thinks, *this winter mind will melt and they will all come back.* The cafe brimful with voices, pipe smoke, wet wool. The child murmuring sums; her father barking headlines, snapping his paper. *Herring for Holland, a councillor on the fiddle, a fisherman on the mend.* Words spill outside, bubble through the cobbles, and he is carried on them, floats high above rooflines. There – once again smoke issues from chimneys, and there, boats laid out on a blue-dome of sea.

The young man leans forward, speaks low of small matters, of money, of business. The woman won't answer.

Hesitation is weakness. This thought comes unbidden. And looking again, he sees only duty, loyalty, each for the other. Hears his brother, his sister declare they are leaving, would die if they stayed, because nothing was left but narrowness, a single way. That final train's whistle, the rattle of anchor chains sold from the pier, the town growing smaller, the voices more shrill. *We are a place in desperate need*, he thinks, *and yet we cannot not hear.*

She is rising, leaving, looking out on the morning when his rusted voice stops her. He will tell of the old times. Of trawlermen, drifters, decks glassy with fish scales; of dances and music, of nights at the Electric. But before he can speak, a leeward wave hits him, pulls him over the gunnels and into the sea. The land heaves behind him, the lights of the town dim. His grip is loosed, the old net slips, writhes away, octopus.

Instead, he asks them their names; and shy at first, and glancing, words, their words reach out across the water's washboard peaks to sweep the slipways, guide him home.

When the cafe bell rings them out into morning, he moves to their table, their warmth, to watch them. Here – they walk through fins of sunlight; and here, cross to the proud Electric. Here, they turn to wave again. *They are here.* Their smiles redouble the dawn.

In Which You Give Me Such Words to End With

Ronda Piszk Broatch

When making a bird with two hands it takes an ounce of promise
and yards of remembrance. I promise that I will only tell you stories
you might take with you in times of dire need. The bloodstream
fed thus will carry you far. At each crossroads, in fields of lavender,

under a sky so vast clouds languish, we stop to clean our rifles
throw away the bullets. Gather up our dearest conveniences,
and tie them to the barrels. What must I do to convince you
that there are yet thirty-seven weeks before the coming winter

that there is still time to plant and cultivate our transience like lovers
storing up treasures to be forgotten along the way. It will be years
and years of birds, yards and miles of walking before what is worth having
comes to our minds, as the prisoner, before smoking his last cigarette

understands that there is more than just a train track, or teasing woman
to grow wings for, where each bullet unpacks its powder like stardust.

The Killing

Denise Ryan

When the tree submits
to the sharpened saw.
Stretching its limbs
in jubilation, its rind
releasing layers of time,
as if the spirit of the dying
trunk was slipping away.
A mephitic breath passes over me.

My rumpled eyelids
refuse to close –
watching the tree cutter
hacking a numinous birch
stooped with age rings.
Its powerful presence
declining, like the pale
radiance of dawn.
Even the startled birds
are denied reason.
Flying back to the gutter
half dressed in light,
their pity cries catching
in their little pink throats.

Learning their womb
of woven twigs,

is an arid cup of sap,
flowing like tumbleweed
along the dusty path.
Leaves run towards
a dead horizon, and red
back beetles rush like blood,
into the mutilated earth.

One Female is a Pen

Deirdre Hines

I told him I found her in the lake.
A necessary lie. I said that she was
drowning
and that an old woman stood beside her,
their bag of wet crumbs, their scent of human
skin
and of the paper some tree had died for
as foul as any festering flyridden corpse
hidden
in our waters by desperate soldiers or lazy farmers –
The girl was in two places, or was of two
faces
at least that's what I thought I truly thought.
Like all reflections not every image was
clear
but when she appeared out from time
to throw her votive bread into these dark
waters
I knew we'd hovered here in Haven
with our golden beaks and obsidian eyes
eternal
too long – and that in that space between
this girl's present and all her future faces one

chance
and one chance only was open to bite down
and open up her left wrist to bind us both
pen and girl
as sabre or palette or word to render real
our kind – too long wanderers to our wetland
shores
fell into all the easy erasures of his ego
with romantic lies like the one about
Leda
or those shirts made in silence of graveyard nettles
and bleeding fingers his charm to block the real
story –
I wanted to let her hitch a ride upon my back
but she had fallen into the old woman's arms
who
peeled the shell from off my firstborn's egg.

Pathways

Marc Swan

It's not poker or blindman's bluff
when you hold something close to your chest
that isn't a secret but you feel secretive.
Transparency can be viewed in many ways.
When the diagnosis is revealed with steps
yet to be heard, the doc sits quietly letting
you absorb. It's not a time for twist and shout,
letting it all out – what out? The unknown.
Options explained in a simple way, few words,
complications understood; the room darkens
then lights up again. There are no road signs
but the path is clear. It narrows down to time,
either on your side, and what that can mean,
or the other option, not quite as clean.

Forever After

Mary Lennon

EARLY FAMILY PHOTOGRAPHS ARE UNRELIABLE – heads missing, feet in focus, or heads in, faces blurry, like we're not fully there. We worked out later that my mother leaned forward when she pressed the button, and Oops went the heads, Oop-la came the feet. Then Caroline, the eldest, took over and there we all are, heads and feet. The last photograph from that time is of my Holy Communion – white dress, veil, bolero, all Caroline's hand-me-downs but shiny white shoes, white lacy socks – all brand new. We're in the back garden, in the merry month of May, Mam holding Stevie, Dad in his suit, me, Ciaran, Sylvie, all there except Caroline who's behind the lens, fixing us in time.

Each of us has an enlarged, framed copy of that photograph, the last one before the bad times. Before our father, well – went missing – is what the Gardaí and the newspapers called it.

Missing, missing, missing.

Saturday afternoon, he went to Whelan's pub with his friend, Joe, to watch Arsenal play. Everyone said he was in good form, then he left to collect his winnings at the bookie's. But he didn't come back, not that day, the next or the weeks, months after. Not forever after.

And for us, everything changed; forever after.

*

Sergeant O'Brien was in charge, he talked to us, the neighbours, to people at Dad's work. Father Frawley called, said we should pray for him. The Gardaí searched with dogs who sniffed Dad's vest and carried his scent: GAA pitches in case he took a walk and fell ... back lanes in case he was robbed, left unconscious ... the canal in case he'd fallen in ... .

Mam and Uncle Jimmy went on TV, which we watched, piled together on the sofa. Mam was crying, 'If you're out there Thomas, please get in touch, please ....'

Joe got neighbours together to search the Dodder banks, a place they used to go fishing. Tireless efforts, the newspapers said.

But *nothing, nothing, nothing*.

Our house was full of empties, empty chair at the table, empty side of Mam and Dad's bed, empty shaving cream, empty tobacco box, empty *Gone fishin* mug – which Caroline hid.

Uncle Jimmy took us for drives on Sunday mornings and Aunt Nancy came Wednesdays to play cards. At school, the principal, our teachers, even the girls and boys came and said, 'Sorry about your dad,' like their mams and dads told them to. Everybody was sorry. Maria Byrne brought me in a skipping rope with flashing handles from her dad's shop.

Sorry, sorry, sorry.

When we went to Mass or the cinema, people who didn't know us, now knew us, because they'd seen us in the newspapers and they stared. *They're the children of the missing man.*

Caroline got annoyed, 'I'm sick of it, they should mind their own business!'

Slowly everyone, except my mother, got tired of searching, looking, hoping. Jimmy and Nancy visited less, Sergeant O'Brien stopped calling, just phoned. There were no clues. Our father had disappeared into thin air. It was around that time we began to call him our father, not Dad anymore.

At school they got tired too, of being sorry. In the yard, Sennan McCabe said, 'E.T. musta got your Dad!' and it moved like wildfire. Some laughed, giggled, others snickered behind their hands, pretending not to be laughing, while me and Sylvie cried and got taken to the principal's office. She gave us tissues to wipe our eyes, KitKat and Fanta to cheer us up, told us that Sennan would be in trouble with her, but he meant no harm, was just being 'thoughtless'!

Thoughtless, thoughtless, thoughtless.

Then Stevie got bronchitis and had to go to hospital and when he came home he had to stay in bed. After school, Mam was lying in the bed with him. 'I can't let him out of my sight,' she said. Then Sylvie got sick, stayed home, the following week me and Ciaran got it, and finally, Caroline too.

'They've all got the flu that's going round,' Mam told the principal on the phone.

Then she put us all in her big bed, top and tailing, and dragged in the single bed from the boxroom for herself. She stayed with us most days, only getting up to boil eggs for breakfast, soup for lunch, sausages and potatoes for dinner. We didn't mind being sick – glad to be away from school, reading comics, playing games and other stuff.

Then, on a Sunday, our grandmother arrived from Ballina. Tommy Lavelle, Mam's cousin, drove her up, stopped for tea and sandwiches and drove back down again. That evening Grandma made our tea and told us we'd been in bed long enough, needed to get our skates on. Sylvie nearly laughed, which would have started us all off, but she held it in.

We went back to school on Monday, in our brushed-down uniforms, and when we came home the house was cleaned, washing hung on the line and a pot of stew was on the stove. Only Mam didn't get up, she just lay in bed, facing the wall, saying she was dead tired. Doctor Brennan came each day for a week to make sure she took her tablets.

Stevie followed Grandma around, moved every time she moved, wouldn't let me or Caroline pick him up. Grandma dandled him on her lap and sang, 'The Yellow Rose of Texas' which he loved and we all sang with her. After a few weeks we got used to Grandma being in charge and Mam got up some evenings.

It was a Saturday – Saturdays are not good days in our family – when Grandma and Mam had their big fight. Only me and Caroline heard it, listening with the bedroom door ajar. Grandma was very cross, telling Mam she'd stayed in bed long enough, couldn't sleep her life away, and Mam kept crying and saying, 'I can't do it, I can't do it.'

Then Grandma shouted, 'Are you going to leave those childer like he did?'

Caroline went stiff next to me, but Grandma hadn't finished. 'You know where they'll end up, don't you? Defenceless in some orphanage!'

The words were splinters of ice, like after Caroline read me *The Ice Queen* story when I was little and I got nightmares. I felt blue with cold, didn't look at Caroline in case she'd frozen too.

Grandma stayed for months while Mam slowly got back on her feet, she called it. And so we escaped the clutches of the Ice Queen and stayed together in our own house.

In time, our story became old news, wore itself out and faded from view.

**

I live in London now where nobody knows – or cares – about missing fathers. Some of my new friends have absent fathers – the ones who don't go missing, just aren't around much. I work in a fashion studio in Covent Garden. They take the mick out of me at home, 'Covent Garden, ooh-la-la,' as though it's Buckingham Palace, but underneath they're pleased. I've worked my ass off since college, interning, waitressing, interning again, to get a one-year contract with CAF – Chloe, Aysha, Franco, 'Three hot, young Brit designers', *The Mail* declared them recently. I fetch, carry, cut, sew, administrate, but I'm learning lots and earn enough to cover rent in a shared house in Peckham and a budget lifestyle. And, I absolutely love London.

Well … loved it until a fortnight ago when I was … mugged on the London Underground.

A Thursday, I left work earlier than usual, got a seat on the train and began people-watching, much harder to do when you're clinging to an overhead rail. The usual cosmopolitan crowd, but my attention was taken by a young boy, engrossed in *Harry Potter and the Philosopher's Stone* who reminded me of my nephew, Cian. He was dressed in a green school uniform, had dark hair, long lashes and was very beautiful. I wanted to sketch him, something I hadn't been doing since college, but how could I without him noticing? He raised his eyes once, sensing my attention – light brown they were – then resumed reading. As the train approached his station, he closed his book and a man sitting further along got up, and together they moved towards the door. I gave the man a cursory glance, greying hair, sixties, grandfather maybe? And, forever after, I won't know why I did it, but I looked at him again and something hot, like a burning rod, jabbed at my chest, and as the doors wheezed open I was on my feet, following them.

They took the escalator and exited onto a busy high street I didn't know. I kept them in sight, stopping to look in shop windows if they slowed, all the time outside of myself, robotic, compelled. For several minutes they walked straight ahead before they entered an Asian supermarket. I stopped, stared into an Oxfam window, seeing only my own white, ghostly face. When they reappeared, the boy had an ice cream cone, the man a newspaper, which he rolled and put into the pocket of his jacket. The movement brought the hot jab to my chest again and I was bent double, had to lean against the cold brick wall to stay on my feet.

I'd gone far enough, I knew it … I'd gone too far … but as if my life depended on it, I straightened up and was following again. But they'd disappeared – and now a scream was building in my throat. Right or left? Right or left? It had to be one or other. But which? Which?

I took the right, onto a long, tree-lined street … and ahead … unbelievably … there they were, still walking. I followed. Then quite quickly, they turned left, onto a shorter street lined with low, mock-Tudor-style houses. I held back, before I turned left too. Halfway down, they went in through a gateway and might have disappeared inside if the man hadn't stopped to fumble for keys. I walked fast, faster, drew close, closer – until I was at the gate.

His back was turned, he didn't see me, might never have seen me, except I spoke.

One word, loudly. 'Dad?'

He heard it; he heard it and froze.

My wise heart began pounding against my ribcage, urging escape from the long, long moment – as he slowly turned to face me. He was ashen, looked aghast with … fear?

'Caroline?'

The voice was familiar from down a long tunnel of faraway, but it had a new sound on it, a London sound.

'Amy.'

Suddenly the boy moved forward, pulled at his sleeve. 'Dad? Are we not going in?'

I'd forgotten the beautiful boy, but his words, like a metallic screech, stunned me and I was going to slide to the ground, be trapped outside that house – forever – unless … unless I ran.

But I couldn't move, was stuck to the pavement, while words from the man were floating towards me, words I couldn't hear, wouldn't hear, not one single word. I grabbed the low wall, held onto it to stagger away, almost falling, then grabbed the next wall, the next, then each wall after, until gasping for air, legs shaking, I limped my way towards the end of that endless street.

***

Mornings, I wake to that picture in the garden, us all smiling in the sun, remember Caroline squinting behind the lens, telling us what to do. Then I touch the cold lump inside my chest and that helps. I get up, go to work as usual. I don't lie facing the wall, I know where that leads.

But I fear for the others – if I tell.

And if I don't tell?

I must make myself unknow it.

As he did.

Now's the Time

Sara Backer

Long ago on the edge of Vienna and lost,
I walk off the map into an alley of sidewalk vendors
squatting beside strange treasure spread on tablecloths:

ebony bracelets carved as snakes, necklaces strung
with silver coins, lace scarves, intricately
painted eggs, porcelain elephants, brass salamanders.

I want everything.
I can't choose.

Then, someone whistles sharply: a six-note riff
I recognize
from Charlie Parker's saxophone.

Vendors roll tablecloths into sacks and run.
The alley instantly empties
down to old bricks with German graffiti.

I stand in the middle of this magic trick
as two policemen walk the beat.

Rubbed Smooth Though Grave to Grave

Simon Perchik

Rubbed smooth though grave to grave
what this rock carries inside helps lift it
to see through – the dress, black

then silence then the shoulders
she was buried in, growing wild
the way every mountain bit by bit

waves goodbye as if its belly
is always empty, needs to be warmed
pulled closer, sleeves and all.

Our Physical Relationship

Heather Christle

Some words take shape
when spoken or thought of
aloud; *cup*, for instance,
corresponds so exactly
with the object it names
that your mind can fill
with them as mine has
this morning: I am a small
cup factory and my skull
is lined with shelves,
my mouth caked with clay.
I don't mean to complain.
Just because a thing is
occurring and unstoppable
does not mean it is bad.
I'm practising a belief
that my crown is an ongoing
sequence of material events,
such as this one and also this.
There is a *wren* in the *jiggling light*.

Oscar Wilde on Merrion Square

Stephen Finucane

He heard the promised rain begin that night.
It told him time was short, he was alone,
and anything or anyone he might
have appealed to must leave him to his own
devices to plot his own unknown course
through unknowable happenstance without
a chart to guide him, debouchment and source
equally and now palpably in doubt.
He heard the promised rain begin that night.
Time proceeded, darkness reigned, his thoughts turned.
The gardens awaited the morning light.
Redemption could occur but not be earned.
Clouds would always fill, rain would always fall.
A shower, a deluge; a tremor, a squall.

Think Before You Flush

Knute Skinner

(a sign in a hotel-room toilet)

What about?
The Alpine route of Hannibal?
Those elephants must have been quite
a challenge.

Or Moses breaking the tablets?
He was human,
was he not?

Or hurling's great goalkeeper
Davy Fitzgerald?
Not very many *sliothars*
got past him.

I think
that that
is enough,
and it's time to flush.

The Entomologist

Mairead Willis

THE AUGUST I GET CROW'S FEET, my mother takes ill, and I drive home to look after her house. I take over for a teacher on maternity leave at the local school, where the seventh and eighth graders together make up one class. *A Tale of Two Cities* is the first book on the syllabus. The students find it boring, and so do I. In the evenings, I sometimes watch my mother peck at Jell-O in the hospital. Usually, though, I have tea with my neighbour, Dr Jericho, the entomologist.

***

Dr Jericho wears large, round glasses which magnify her eyes to three times their actual size. Every day she wears a different iridescent, multicoloured shawl. Her movements are choppy and too quick. As a child I was afraid of her, but now she is old and nearly bald. I enjoy spending time with her because, unlike my mother, she speaks.

'Well, Amanda, how is your mother these days?'

'No change, Dr Jericho.'

'Strange for a woman to clam up at her age.'

'It was a dry summer, and her flower garden died. The doctors think that might be to blame.'

'Yes. I came across a colony of bees once – have I told you this one?'

'I don't think so.'

'They were in Walla Walla, Washington – scrumptious onions there, you know. When their queen began to die, they all cleared out of the hive and left her alone. Unusual behaviour.'

'Is it really?'

'Very. Anyway, the people in Walla Walla turned all their fields to onion farms. The wildflower population decreased, and the bees all but disappeared.'

'Were you able to save any?'

'Of course, all I had to do was plant more wildflowers.'

***

I creep around my mother's hospital room like a teenager trying to sneak out at night. Any small cough or misstep I make seems to interrupt some delicate equilibrium only she can sense. Once, though I am barely breathing so as to preserve the silence, she wakes and winces when she sees me. I realise later that it is because my handbag is too red.

***

My students can't decide whether or not they like the guillotine. They enjoy the knitted hit list. To be murdered for the sake of one's love, they do not like.

'What would Lucie have to do to deserve Sydney's sacrifice?' I ask.

'She just needs to be, you know, a little more *there*,' says Chloe, who wears more scrunchies on her wrist than anyone else. The others agree, and then they debate whether your head can still think for a while after it is chopped off. I decide the conversation is appropriate as it is very scientific.

***

'A cockroach can live for a week without its head, but then it dies of thirst,' says Dr Jericho.

'Doesn't it need a brain?'

'The name of the game is to survive and reproduce, Amanda, and most insects out-compete us by a mile with hardly any brain. Have you reproduced, young lady?'

'No, Dr Jericho. Have you?'

'I have one son.' Her spectacles glitter.

'How many offspring does a cockroach have?'

'Two to three hundred.'

***

In class we are all asking ourselves whether one action can redeem a life. The Christian students think so. I ask them if Lucie is saved.

'How?' asks Peter, whose hair is always slicked down with something like engine oil.

'She gives birth, isn't that a good act?'

'No, Miss, we mean, like, really good.'

***

I transplant a clump of milkweed growing through the cracked playground asphalt to a pot, and I put the pot on my mother's windowsill. She winces less. The next day, the nurses take it away because aphids are roaming the petals. She winces more.

***

'You're wilting,' says Dr Jericho.

'I don't know what to do about my mother.'

'Those hospital staff don't know squat about living.' Dr Jericho has lain dormant in the hospital before and is an expert on the subject.

'I can't revive the rose bushes. It's too hot now and it'll be too cold later.'

'The secret to this new climate is indoor horticulture.' She wags a segmented finger at me. 'Plant bushes in the basement and install some LED lights. And you know what else you need?'

'A manual?'

'Pollinators!' She takes a wooden pillbox with a brass clasp from atop the china cabinet and hands it over.

When I lift the lid, I gasp and nearly drop the box. Inside lies a butterfly preserved. Its wings are orange with leopard spotting and a hospital-gown-blue border. In some places the colour has flaked away, laying bare a flossy scaffold like the veins of a leaf. Long, fawn-coloured hairs stretch from the body to the innermost wings. It shifts when my hand shakes, and I am afraid it may spring up and fly away. I didn't know death could be so incandescent.

'That's to look at, not to keep,' says Dr Jericho.

***

The last day of September is so hot that the leaves appear to have tanned rather than expired. The class and I take a break from the French Revolution to go butterfly hunting on the playground. Veronica, who cries during spelling tests, manages to catch one. She jumps up and down in excitement, and I warn her not to crush it between her cupped palms.

***

Dr Jericho falls and cracks her hip. As the paramedics load her onto the ambulance, she curses the frailty of her endoskeleton. Two days later, her son arrives, and I help him choose specimens to decorate her ward. He is handsome, and married.

***

The doctors decide that silence is not an illness, and my mother is discharged. I give her my arm and guide her to the car. She is light as a ladybug, wrapped in a blouse with a lily motif. We would move faster if I carried her.

***

I stay with my mother until the full-time teacher returns in January. The class and I read *To Kill a Mockingbird*, which everyone prefers. One day, when I am off for Thanksgiving weekend, I see my mother pause in the doorway to the basement, her face awash in pink from the grow lights. Since the addition of the butterflies, the bushes have grown like gangbusters, sending branches crawling up the handrail. My mother shuffles down the stairs, humming.

Something Happened

Richard W. Halperin

A good formal poem about Brent geese
Passes through my hand. The way they rise
Above the DART tracks outside Greystones.
Then, something happened – happens – to the poem.
Why am I writing it? What am I about? Better
To see the geese again in my mind's eye.
My hand continues, the poem not written,
It can mean something only to myself,
The wreck of my life at that time, friends
In Greystones, something knitting together.
What is a poem? What is a day? A jumble
Of DNA or gyres or – suddenly –
Aquerò in Lourdes and – suddenly – not.
Brent geese. That they rose. Something happened.

Forced

Barbara E. Hunt

Don't our choicest red
rhubarb stalks rocket
in brooding blackness

cloistered from hardening-off
bestowed by meagre
gardens

where begging for slanted sun
in spring's cold snap strands them
sour, green and threaded tough.

But warehoused, these slither
supple to sweet and tender
whispers; grousing, groaning

day and night; all raucous ruby
racing, so's to make any
green-grocer blush.

Things To Learn About Life While Blackberry Picking

Neil Banks

The ripe berries are there but sometimes you have to look more than once.
Move around, push leaves aside, vary your angle of approach.
Often these methods will reveal hidden gifts.

Often the best fruits are in the hardest to reach places –
that's life.
Sometimes there are fine ripe berries in easy reach –
that's life too.

There's nothing wrong with just picking what's in front of you
and avoiding the distraction of what's over there.
Just pick at your own pace and concentrate on picking well.
It isn't a competition. All we collect will end up in the same pot.
But it's still a competition. Biggest, fastest, bestest, et cetera.
What level you choose to engage with this at is up to you.

Brambles are viciously thorny so be careful.
Try as you might to touch only the berries,
those sharp little thorns will sometimes catch you.
Sometimes, for the right fruit, it's worth suffering these scratches and worse.
Other times, however, it is not. Try to learn how to tell the difference.

There will be times when you've gathered a palmful of berries and instead of tipping
them into the pot you go for just one more and the whole lot drops from your hand
and is lost. All you can do is carry on, start again with the one berry left between your
finger and thumb, though perhaps this is a good one to just eat on the spot.
When such mishaps occur be careful for a while, but don't be too careful too long.

When you've picked as much in one place as you want, or as much as you can,
move on in search of the next spot – don't linger.
And don't pick the whole place clean either. Leave some for the birds,
for the pickers after you. There is such a thing as enough.

If other people come along you can stand your ground within reason.
If your picking is threatened there will be several options open to you,
but war should be the absolute last of these.

Appreciate this time of closeness to whoever's picking with you,
even if it's only you and your shadow.
Use the berries well. Bake tarts, crumbles, whatever.
Share your bounty.
And make jam, if only so that the day's picking
and all that's in it –
this communion with nature –
may be preserved
and months from now be instantly recalled
with the simple
lick
of a spoon.

Greenhouse

Billy Fenton

It's something you always wanted
but never had. When the hedge is up,
we'll put one in, you used to say.
Today the man came, a damp Saturday
in January, a cold shivering day.
Four hours later you had your wish.

After he left, I went to the garden.
You are there as clear as day,
in the centre of your new greenhouse.
The light of summer around you.
The climb of plants about you.
You pop a tomato between your
teeth, put your arms around me,
pass it into my mouth.
I close my eyes, feel your mouth
on mine, the taste of you
on my tongue, the sweetness
of tomato as I bite.

When I open my eyes,
the greenhouse is gleaming new,
but empty.
Where did you go?
Where did you plant your box of wishes?
So I can fill this greenhouse up with new life,
fill it up with the beat of your heart.

Textiles

Adam Hughes

Do not wear clothing woven of two kinds of material. – Leviticus 19:19

And do not cross two different mountains
while wearing the same shoes; and do not
brush your teeth after drinking orange juice;
and do not listen to two different songs
while trying to sing a third; and do not
dream with two desires, only one
which cannot come true; and do not sleep
with your feet sticking out from under
the blankets as this is an abomination
and shows a lack of consistency;
and do not wonder which way the other
road goes because the scenery there
may be better or worse than the scenery here
but it is there and you are here; and do not try
to understand the difference between
a crow and a raven and a rook as they
are all black birds that eat dead things
and sometimes you don't need to split feathers;
and do not try to see two different things
with your two different eyes; and do not
offer your hand to someone who is willing to take it;

and do not follow someone who wants to lead you;
and do not swim between the beacons
but only in waters that threaten
to obliterate you and sail you a thousand
miles from shore, a waterlogged vessel
with minimal navigational equipment;
and do not pop two different kinds
of popcorn in the same popper; and do not
make two of the same promises
to two different people; and do not
weave two hearts together,
instead plant them in neat rows
next to one another and if the wind
is serene and the rain doesn't chase
its own tail and the sun overcomes
its own arrogance and the rabbits and the birds
their gluttony and the gardener is not distracted,
then the hearts will weave themselves
and you'll never know what material they used.

Look Into My Eyes

Ruth Knafo Setton

LOOK INTO MY EYES, HE SAID, and I did, and I saw the promise of everything I wanted to believe and he was there and beautiful and true the way I'd dreamed and when he said you were thinking of a castle on the sand, I said yes, and when he said you were thinking of heavy gold sand, the kind that feels wet and thick even when it's dry, I said yes, and then he said you were thinking of Tunisia — no, that's not it — North Africa — wait, it's coming to me, don't say anything, give me your hand, let me feel where you are right now and I gave him my hand and his felt large and strong, but more than that it felt hot, burning hot, and I stepped back in shock and then it pulsed against mine and I stepped back again and he said, please don't be afraid, people are always afraid, but it's only me, it's only me, and he bent close to me and said, ah, not Tunisia, not Morocco, but Algeria, and I said yes oh god yes, and he laughed as delighted as a child and I laughed too and for a moment I forgot that his hand was still gripping mine, and without turning his head he asked his assistant to read what I had written on the card behind him and the assistant said in a ringing voice, a church bell voice, the woman wrote Algeria, and the audience cheered and applauded and I looked into his eyes even though I admit I was afraid, by then I was really afraid, but I'll tell you what I saw as precisely as I can so you won't accuse me of lying or pretending, this is what I saw: eyes like black coffee glinting with the depths of water, almost transparent, glowing with life-force and excitement and delight, and suddenly my fear changed to amazement, and he knew, he felt the change instantly, and his hand, maybe the strongest hand I'd ever felt squeezed a message into mine, pressed, *impressed* on my palm one word, and I knew he was waiting for me to say it, the word he was passing to me, and I heard the audience gasp as if they were all one person, and I swear I heard their hearts beat but it was more like ticking than beating, a thousand clocks ticking at once, and he squeezed harder until my hand ached with the pain of not living up to this dream, this need to understand and know, to transcend the flesh and truly connect with another human being, and he was a human being, that's what he was telling me with the pressure of his hand, with his glinting eyes that squinted with the effort, and my bare arm tingled, it was a hot summer night after all, and earlier I'd noticed the theatre was crammed with people, yet there was no air conditioning, and what had dizzied me when I first entered was the smell of human sweat, we were all humans in this room, all sweating, all leaning toward him, but I was the only one holding his hand sizzling with heat and power, I was the one chosen from all the thousands, and still he held my hand and didn't rush me, didn't show impatience, didn't frown or glare the way so many do because I am slow, I understand so little, I see partially, brokenly, and he squeezed and smiled and stared, and I grew courageous and I squeezed and smiled and stared back, and finally he spoke and all he said was tell me, and I didn't ask because it was clear he wanted me to tell him his word but I was still so full of my word, my Algeria, my sand castle heavy golden sand filtering between my fingers and toes, and my nostrils burned and stung from the sweat and the prickles on my upper arm, the arm of the hand he held, as if a mosquito pricked and crawled down my sweating hot flesh, but I couldn't turn my eyes from his, I couldn't lift my hand away, oh no, it belonged to him now, and I smelled the salt sting of the sea, a sea I'd never been to, never swam in, never tasted, never gulped, never waded, and I wondered what made me say Algeria, what made me dream of a castle in the sand, that famous dream shared by so many and shattered by so many, and why did I want to cry now, why did I taste tears in the back of my throat and on my tongue, and he pressed my hand harder and harder until I yelped in pain and he said tell me and I smelled the sea and sweat and tasted tears and my eyes burned and stung tears and he said tell me now, and I said oh god, salt, and he laughed and I tasted his laugh and it was bitter like salt but sweet the way salt is too, sometimes, and when I heard the roar, deafening behind me, the audience screaming, I knew the assistant must have held up the sign he'd written before and I didn't have to look to know he'd written SALT and he said look into my eyes, and very softly, my love, and no one heard but me, the way no one had heard his soul cry out salt but me, and I looked but I couldn't see because tears filled my eyes and my throat, and he released my hand and I almost fell from the shock, the sudden cold after the blazing hot sweaty room and suddenly I was cold and alone in a freezing room of strangers and I cried look at me but he had already turned and I said my love.

But he was gone.

The Crannóg Questionnaire

Niamh Boyce

How would you introduce yourself as a writer to those who may not know you?

I've published two novels, *The Herbalist* and *Her Kind*, both of which were based on real life trials, the most recent, *Her Kind*, was inspired by the sorcery trial of Alice Kytler. I've also published a poetry collection, *Inside the Wolf*, and write short stories. Though my novels are historical, and combine fact and fiction, most of my other writing is contemporary, and a little more surreal.

When did you start writing?

I've written since I can remember. Notebooks were where I reflected, ranted, drew, played with ideas, wrote poems, cleared my head, puzzled, made lists, promises, resolutions. Though I wrote nightly and read constantly, I never considered publishing anything, or really saw what I was doing as writing at all. I often wrote poems, to try and catch moments, make sense of feelings. I worked with images mostly, and alternated between writing poems and making painting to explore the same subject. This practice was something that stayed at the edge of my life, something I fitted in around everything else. Writing for real, or writing in a definite focused way, didn't happen until 2008 after workshops with John MacKenna. I began writing short stories, and became hooked. John is a brilliant writer and a generous writing teacher.

That was a pivotal time creatively. *Crannóg* published *Wild Cats Buffet* in 2009 – it was my first published story. I was thrilled.

Do you have a writing routine?

It varies according to my workload, but I prefer to write in the morning nowadays. I used to be a night writer – I could work till 4 am writing – but I smoked back then, and I think that helped keep me going. If I have to, I'll write late into the night, but I prefer to get the work done early, otherwise I'll be anxious that something will happen to stop me getting to the work. With novels, I write first drafts into a notebook, and type it up later. With stories, I tend to work on the laptop. If everything is going well, I will make new work early in the day, and I research in the evenings.

When you write, do you picture somehow a potential audience or do you just write?

For a first draft – I don't think of a reader. I try not to think at all. I avoid having an 'idea' – and just write. My aim with writing at this stage is to surprise myself, to drift and remain uncensored. I don't worry about quality, or sense, or coherence. I thoroughly enjoy this stage, there is such potential, the work could be anything, go anywhere. Once the early draft is complete, I leave it aside, and then pick it up a few weeks later. At this stage, the only reader I have in mind is myself – so I revise for sense, get to know the characters better, rework scenes. I enjoy this stage too. Then there's the phase when I (mistakenly) think the novel is finished, and I print it out and read it with A Reader in mind. That's when I regret the fact that I don't plot and I wonder what in hell was I fecking thinking creating such chaos, and wonder will I ever find the story, or make sense of what I have written. I do not enjoy this stage. It is usually the longest and most challenging part of the process. That's when I go looking for inspirational quotes, and make diagrams, and list chapters, and list all the scenes I forgot to write, that a reader will need if they are ever going to make sense of the book.

Some writers describe themselves as planners, while others plunge right in to the writing. Would you consider yourself a planner or a plunger?

I am a plunger. I cannot plan. I have tried to. After the process described above, I once outlined a whole novel – character arcs, story arcs, chapters etc ... once I had done that, I had zero interest in writing it.

How important are names to you in your books? Do you choose the names based on liking the way they sound or for the meaning? Do you have any name-choosing resources you recommend?

That's interesting – in terms of my novels, they're real characters mixed with fictional ones. With *Her Kind*, I kept the names of the six or so real people who were involved in the sorcery trial. Alice Kytler, Bassilia, Arnold Le Poer, Richard Ledrede, etc … but with Petronella, who is central – I wanted to distinguish my fictional character from the real woman, in my own mind. I'm not entirely sure why, but I needed to do that to be able to write her story. I called my character Petronelle rather than Petronella. It was a tiny change, one letter – but it freed me creatively. I also used fourteenth-century sources to become familiar with the names of the times – the Liber Primus Kilkennius was very useful.

Is there a certain type of scene that's harder for you to write than others? Love? Action? Erotic?

The suffering of women has often been an aesthetic exercise in literary fiction. A complete lack of anger, combined with exquisite suffering seems to be their lot. Because I love words, and images and metaphors – I had to examine that aspect of *Her Kind* and ask myself, 'am I making it beautiful?' Because it's not beautiful.

Tell us a bit about your non-literary work experience please.

I have worked as an indexer, a chambermaid, factory worker, a researcher, a housing advice officer, a social policy officer, a community development worker, a community arts tutor and a librarian.

What do you like to read in your free time?

I love non-fiction that reads like fiction. *The Suspicions of Mister Whicher*, by Kate Summerscale was compelling. *The Darkened Room*, by Alex Owen is an excellent book on Spiritualism. *Montaillou* is a fascinating look at the fourteenth-century inquisition records of Jacques Fournier. P.V Glob's *The Bog People* is so moving and lyrical – Heaney was influenced by it. Fiction-wise, I loved Ali Smith's *Artful*, which weaves lectures on writing with a ghost story. I stay up through the night with Yrsa Sigurdadóttir's crime novels. I was really struck by *Pond* by Claire Louise Bennett. And *Drive Your Plough Over the Bones of the Dead* by Olga Tokarczuk is just fantastic.

What one book do you wish you had written?

None, to be honest – but if I had to choose, it would be Angela Carter's story *The Tiger's Bride*, from her collection *The Bloody Chamber*.

Do you see writing short stories as practice for writing novels?

They are different creatures, aren't they? Not all novelists can write a decent short story, and not all short story writers can, or want to, write novels. Writing short stories isn't practice, or a warm-up for the work of writing a novel – but because they require such attention to word choice and structure and scenes selection, I think writing them, or even trying to write them, will improve a writer.

Do you think writers have a social role to play in society or is their role solely artistic?

That's tricky. I have complicated and contradictory thoughts on that one. 1. I don't think there can be such a thing as 'solely' artistic. Nothing is apolitical. To declare yourself apolitical is to align yourself with the status quo, with those in power. 2. I don't want a social role in terms of my creative work. I want to write whatever comes. But whatever comes is often about power, and that's political. 3. I hate the idea of having an agenda, I think it corrupts the creative instinct. 4. I can't declare that I have no agenda, as (see above) 'nothing is apolitical.' 5. The role Irish artists have played in the past few years has been inspiring and brought change to our society. 6. I guess artists have a social role to play.

Tell us something about your latest publication, please.

My novel *Her Kind* has just been published by Penguin Random House. It's a reimagining of The sorcery trial of Alice Kytler that occurred in fourteenth-century Kilkenny. The case was a landmark case in the history of the witchcraft trials, predating the European witchcraft trials by two hundred years. It's been called an 'atmospheric magical thriller' by Hilary A. White in the *Sunday Independent*. It was shortlisted for the EU Prize for Literature; the judges called it 'as searing a critique of our own time as Arthur Miller's *The Crucible*'.

Can writing be taught?

I believe it should be taught, and taught to everyone at a young age. It's a tool. A mode of expression.

1. I think creativity is there for anyone to tap into, that there is healing and transformation to be accessed and that writing or art isn't the

exclusive property of the talented. I think anyone who enjoys writing should write, and relish it.

2. Not everyone writes well, and even those who can write well often don't have what it takes to create a publishable story, or to finish a novel. There is the private realm, where we write for ourselves, or for a few – and there is the public realm, where we consider publication, authorship.

3. One does not have to automatically follow the other. If, by writing, we mean writing for publication, writing to become an author, only so much can be taught. Lots of people have talent, what they don't always have is the persistence, and a strong enough desire to tell their stories.

Have you given or attended creative writing workshops and if you have share your experiences a bit please?

Before I began to write, I was a facilitator with a community development background – and I think that was a help when I began to teach writing workshops. I've taught creative writing for beginners, novel writing, fact to fiction, short story writing, etc ... I really enjoy this aspect of being a writer, especially when working on my Fact to Fiction courses. It seems to suit how my personality works. I really love seeing people tap into their creativity. I like discussing the nuts and bolts of fiction. I enjoy getting a lot done, in working intensively. We always write together. I think that's important. There's a magic that happens, when people write together. I came to writing myself through a writing workshop, so I think they have the potential to be transformative. Libraries often run free creative writing workshops, where they pay the writer, and people participate at no cost to themselves. So workshops are much more accessible than a longer course.

Flash fiction: how driven is the popularity of this form by social media like Twitter and its word limits? Do you see Twitter as somehow leading to shorter fiction?

It's hard to know, isn't it? Would flash exist without social media? I think so, it predates it – but the popularity is probably linked to our use of devices, and our shorter attention spans. I don't know if Twitter leads to shorter fiction, it seems to lead to shorter tempers. I've only begun to use it properly myself – so I don't have much of an insight into its ways.

Finally what question do you wish that someone would ask about your writing, and how would you answer it?

This doesn't apply here, but ... When *The Herbalist* came out, I sometimes felt like wearing a big fake moustache (on panels in particular) so people might mistake me for a Writer, and ask me about the actual writing (form, language, style, sentences or use of images, metaphors, anything …) instead of asking me, so very often, about Gender, about the fact of being a 'Woman' writer, about writing strong 'Female' characters. When I was published back in 2013, I was quite surprised by this, at how my novel about a person coming of age was not seen as a universal story, in the way books by writers who didn't need fake moustaches were.

Finally, finally some Quick Pick Questions:
E-books or print?
Print every time.
Dog or cat?
Dog every time.
Reviews – read or don't read?
Read.
Best city to inspire a writer: London, Dublin, New York (Other)?
Paris
Favourite meal out: breakfast, lunch, dinner?
Lunch.
Weekly series or box sets?
Neither. The cinema.
Favourite colour?
Red.
Rolling Stones or Beatles?
The Beatles.
Night or day?
Night.

Artist's Statement

Cover image: *Charon*
by Róisín Coyle

Róisín Coyle's work is situated between fact and fiction. She is particularly interested in the Irish folkloric notion of *Idiráit* (between place): a parallel universe, the merging of the real and unreal and an insight into the Irish relationship to the non-rational and how this has affected (infiltrated) people's lives and psyches.
www.roisincoyle.com

<u>Biographical Details</u>

Gail Anderson was shortlisted for the 2018 Bridport Prize (Flash), won the 2018 Winchester Writers' Festival Poetry and Memoir Prizes, and placed second in the 2018 Fish Publishing Flash Fiction competition. Her short fiction, nonfiction and poetry have been published in the *Aesthetica Creative Writing Annual*, *The Southampton Review*, *Strix*, *Litro* and elsewhere. She has worked as a stop-motion animator, musical instrument repair technician and graphic designer.

Sara Backer recently earned an MFA at Vermont College of Fine Arts. She has two poetry chapbooks: *Scavenger Hunt* (2018) and *Bicycle Lotus* (2015). www.sarabacker.com

Neil Banks has had stories and poems featured in *New Irish Writing*, *Crannóg*, *The Stinging Fly*, *The Shot Glass Journal*, *Burning Bush 2* and on RTÉ radio.

Laura Treacy Bentley is a novelist and poet from Huntington, West Virginia. She is the author of a chapbook/artbook, *Looking for Ireland: An Irish Appalachian Pilgrimage* (2017), a psychological thriller set in Ireland, *The Silver Tattoo* (2013), a short story prequel, *Night Terrors* (2015), and a poetry collection, *Lake Effect* (2006). She was featured on *A Prairie Home Companion* and in *Poetry Daily* and *O Magazine*. lauratreacybentley.com

Ronda Piszk Broatch is the author of *Lake of Fallen Constellations* (MoonPath Press, 2015). She is the recipient of an Artist Trust GAP Grant, and her poems have been nominated for the Pushcart prize. Her journal publications include *Blackbird*, *Prairie Schooner*, *Crannóg*, *Sycamore Review*, *Mid-American Review*, and Public Radio KUOW's *All Things Considered*. She is also a poet and photographer.

Laura Ann Caffrey is a teacher and poet. She has been published in various magazines including *Crannóg*, *The Stinging Fly* and *The Galway Review*. She was shortlisted for the 2018 Cúirt New Writing prize.

Heather Christle is the author of four poetry collections: *Heliopause* and *What is Amazing* are both published by Wesleyan University Press, and *The Trees The Trees* and *The Difficult Farm* are both published by Octopus Books. New poems have recently appeared or are forthcoming in *Granta*, *London Review of Books*, *The New Yorker*, *Poetry*, and elsewhere. Her first book of nonfiction, *The Crying Book*, will be published by Catapult Books in the US and Hanser in Germany this autumn, and by Corsair/Little Brown UK early next year.

Catriona Clutterbuck's poetry has appeared in *Cyphers*, *Oxford Poetry*, *Oxford Poets 2007: An Anthology*, *Poetry Ireland Review*, *The Blue Nib*, *The Honest Ulsterman*, *The May Anthology of Oxford and Cambridge Poetry*, and *Windows Authors and Artist Introductions Series*. Her work was selected for Poetry Ireland

Introductions Readings in 2006, and has been shortlisted for the Trim Poetry Prize (2019). A chapbook, *Ghosts in my Heels*, was published in 2005. She lives in Co. Tipperary.

Billy Fenton writes poetry and short stories. His work has been published in *The Irish Times*, *Poetry Ireland Review*, and *Cattails*. He was shortlisted for a Hennessy Award in 2018.

Cian Ferriter recently completed an Arvon poetry course. He lives in Dublin.

Stephen Finucane works in adult education, delivering courses to unemployed adults. He taught in an inner-London comprehensive school for seven years and has also lived and taught in Germany and Cyprus. He has an MA in Anglo-Irish Literature from University College Dublin.

Mary Melvin Geoghegan has five collections of poetry published, her most recent, *As Moon and Mother Collide*,with Salmon Poetry (2018). Her work has been widely published including in *Poetry Ireland Review*, *The Sunday Times*, *The Stinging Fly*, *The Moth*, *The Stony Thursday Book*, *Crannóg*, *Skylight 47*, *Orbis 184*, *Hodges Figgis 250th Anthology* (2018), *Poems on the DART* (2018), *Cyphers*, amongst others. She won the Longford Festival Award for Poetry in 2013, and was shortlisted in 2015 for the Cúirt New Writing prize and the Francis Ledwidge Poetry Award. In 2017 she was shortlisted for The Fish Poetry Award, The Rush Poetry Award and for the Padraic Colum Poetry Prize in 2018. She is a member of the Writers in Schools Scheme with Poetry Ireland and had edited several anthologies of children's poetry.

Richard W. Halperin's fourth collection from Salmon is *Catch Me While You Have the Light* (2018). His ninth collection for Lapwing is *Luna Moth & Jacob's Ladder* (2019).

Kevin Higgins is co-organiser of Over The Edge literary events in Galway, Ireland. He teaches poetry workshops at Galway Arts Centre, Creative Writing at Galway Technical Institute, and is Creative Writing Director for the National University of Ireland – Galway Summer School. He is poetry critic of *The Galway Advertiser*. His poetry is discussed in *The Cambridge Introduction to Modern Irish Poetry* and features in *Identity Parade: New British and Irish Poets* (ed. Roddy Lumsden, Bloodaxe, 2010) and in *The Hundred Years' War: Modern War Poems* (ed. Neil Astley, Bloodaxe, April 2014). In 2014 his poetry was the subject of a paper 'The Case of Kevin Higgins, or, The Present State of Irish Poetic Satire' presented by David Wheatley at a Symposium on Satire at the University of Aberdeen. *The Selected Satires of Kevin Higgins* was published by NuaScéalta in 2016; a pamphlet of his political poems *The Minister For Poetry Has Decreed* was published also in 2016 by Culture Matters, imprint of the UK-based Manifesto Press. *The Stinging Fly* magazine described him as 'likely the most read living poet in Ireland'. He has published five collections of poetry with Salmon, most recently *Song of Songs 2.0: New & Selected Poems* (2017). His next poetry collection, *Sex and Death at Merlin Park Hospital*, is published by Salmon Poetry (June 2019).

Deirdre Hines is an award-winning poet and playwright. Her first book of poems *The Language of Coats* includes the poems which won The Listowel Poetry Collection Prize. She has been shortlisted in The Allingham Poetry Prize 2018 and The Kavanagh Poetry Prize 2011, and longlisted in The Gregory O'Donohue 2013. New poems have appeared in *The Bombay Review, Abridged, Boyne Berries, NWW magazine, Crannóg, The Lake, Three Drops from a Cauldron* and elsewhere. She reviews poetry for *Sabotage* and *Riggwelter*. She sits on the organisational committee of North West Words.

Adam Hughes is the author of four full-length poetry collections, most recently *Allow the Stars To Catch Me When I Rise* (Salmon Poetry, 2017) and *Deep Cries Out to Deep* (Aldrich Press, 2017). Born and raised in Central Ohio, he now resides in the foothills of Virginia's Blue Ridge Mountains where he is pursuing an MFA at Randolph College.

Barbara E. Hunt has been published in e-zines, journals, anthologies and magazines in North America, the UK, Europe and Australia. Her poetry/colouring book, *Devotions* (2017) recently won the Calgary Poetry Contest.

Maria Kenny's short stories and flash fiction have appeared in journals in Ireland, the UK and Mexico. She was longlisted for the WOW! award in 2016, highly rated in the Maria Edgeworth Short Story competition in 2018 and was shortlisted for the Kanturk Flash Fiction Competition in 2019. She is also a featured writer for the online journal *The Casket of Fictional Delights*. She is currently editing her second novel. @mpkenny1000

Mary Lennon writes fiction. poetry and non-fiction. She co-authored *Across the Water: Irish Women's Emigration to Britain*, published by Virago. She was a runner-up in the Sean O'Faoláin competition. She was shortlisted and longlisted for the Fish competition and the Colm Tóibín competition and won the Listowel Poetry Prize. She teaches Creative Writing in Dublin.

Kirsten McKenzie is a writer living and working in Fife, Scotland. She has published two novels and several short stories in various literary magazines.

Tatjana Mirkov-Popovicki lives in Canada where she emigrated from Serbia in the nineties. Her work has received awards in Canada and has been published in the USA by New Rivers Press and Momaya Press.

Deborah Moffatt's second collection, *Eating Thistles*, will be published by Smokestack Books in August; a collection in Scottish Gaelic is forthcoming. She has won prizes for her poetry in both languages, including a WOW! Award and the Wigtown Poetry Competition.

Simon Perchik is an attorney whose poems have appeared in *Partisan Review, Forge, Poetry, Osiris, The New Yorker* and elsewhere. His most recent collection is *The Osiris Poems* published by boxofchalk, 2017. Free e-books and his essay *Magic,*

Illusion and Other Realities can be viewed at www.simonperchik.com and an interview at https://www.youtube.com/watch?v=MSK774rtfx8.

Ria Collins has been published in *Skylight 47*, *A New Ulster*, *Bangor Literary Journal*, and *Poethead*. She was shortlisted for Over the Edge New Writer of the Year in 2016 and longlisted in 2017 and 2018. She was shortlisted for Poems for Patience in 2017 and 2018, and shortlisted for Bray Literary Festival poetry competition in 2018. She performed a collaboration of her work with music at the Cúirt International Festival of Literature in 2018.

Denise Ryan has ben published in *THE SHOp*, *Crannóg*, and in several online journals. She was highly commended, shortlisted and runner-up in several poetry competitions such as the Francis Ledwidge and the Jonathan Swift awards. Between 2010 and 2013, she was selected to write a series of poems for the National Famine Commemoration. Her first book, *Of Silken Waters,* was published in autumn 2017 by Ara Pacis Publishers (Chicago, USA).

Ruth Knafo Setton is the author of the novel *The Road to Fez*. She is the recipient of fellowships and awards from the National Endowment of the Arts, Pennsylvania Council on the Arts, PEN, *Writer's Digest*, *The Saturday Evening Post*, *Cutthroat*, and *Nimrod*. Her poetry, fiction, and creative nonfiction have been nominated for Pushcart Prizes and have appeared in many journals and anthologies, including *Tiferet*, *The North American Review*, *The Jerusalem Post*, *The Literary Traveler*, *Arts & Letters*, *Women Writing Desire*, *Becoming Myself: Reflections on Growing Up Female,* and *Best Contemporary Jewish Writing*. Her first screenplay was a finalist in numerous screenwriting competitions, including the Sundance Screenwriters' Lab. A former Fiction Editor of *Arts & Letters,* she has taught Creative Writing at Lehigh University and on Semester at Sea.

Beate Sigriddaughter is poet laureate of Silver City, New Mexico, USA, 2017–2019. Her work has received several Pushcart Prize nominations and poetry awards. In 2018 two of her books were published, *Xanthippe and Her Friends* (FutureCycle Press) and *Postcards to a Young Unicorn* (Salador Press). www.sigriddaughter.net.

Knute Skinner's poetry has appeared widely in Ireland, Britain, Australia and North America. He is the author of sixteen books of verse including a collected edition, *Fifty Years: Poems 1957–2007*, which appeared from Salmon. A memoir, *Help Me to a Getaway*, was published by Salmon in 2010. His most recent book is *The Life That I Have* (Salmon Poetry, 2018).

Marc Swan's poems have recently been published or are forthcoming in *Atlanta Review, Ropes, Last Call Anthology, Chiron Review,* among others. *today can take your breath away,* his fourth collection, was published in 2018 by Sheila-Na-Gig Editions.

Susan Tepper's stories, poems, interviews and essays have been published extensively worldwide. An award-winning author, she has been nominated multiple times for the Pushcart Prize and once for a Pulitzer Prize. *Let's Talk,* her column at

Black Heart Magazine, runs monthly. FIZZ, her reading series at KGB Bar, NYC, has been ongoing for eight years.

Mairead Willis is a poetry and fiction writer from Portland, Oregon. Her work has appeared in *Caveat Lector* and *Quarryman*. She is currently pursuing an MA in Creative Writing at University College Cork.

Máiríde Woods has been writing poetry and short stories for many years and has been published in reviews and anthologies. Her stories won Hennessy and Francis MacManus Awards in the 1990s. Her last collection, published with *Astrolabe*, is *A Constant Elsewhere of the Mind*.

Stay in touch with
Crannóg
@
www.crannogmagazine.com